Ripley's Believe It or Not!

Developed and produced by Ripley Publishing Ltd

This edition published and distributed by:

Mason Crest
370 Reed Road, Broomall, Pennsylvania 19008
www.masoncrest.com

Printed and bound in the United States of America.

First printing
9 8 7 6 5 4 3 2 1

Ripley's Believe It or Not!
Startling Art
ISBN-13: 978-1-4222-2572-1 (hardcover)
ISBN-13: 978-1-4222-9247-1 (e-book)
Ripley's Believe It or Not!—Complete 16 Title Series
ISBN-13: 978-1-4222-2560-8

Library of Congress Cataloging-in-Publication Data

Startling art.
    pages cm
ISBN 978-1-4222-2572-1 (hardcover) — ISBN 978-1-4222-2560-8 (series hardcover) —
ISBN 978-1-4222-9247-1 (ebook)
1. Arts—Miscellanea. 2. Curiosities and wonders.
NX67.P74 2012
700—dc23
                    2012020344

PUBLISHER'S NOTE
While every effort has been made to verify the accuracy of the entries in this book, the Publisher's cannot be held responsible for any errors contained in the work. They would be glad to receive any information from readers.

WARNING
Some of the stunts and activities in this book are undertaken by experts and should not be attempted by anyone without adequate training and supervision.

Ripley's Believe It or Not!

Disbelief and Shock!

STARTLING ART

www.MasonCrest.com

STARTLING ART

Artistic license. Who said you need a paintbrush

and paper to create fantastic art? This book proves

amazing creations can be made out of anything!

Gaze in awe at the beautiful tortilla paintings,

the Etch-a-Sketch® masterpieces, and the car

made out of cardboard.

Jeff Gagliardi's amazing Etch A Sketch®
portrait of Leonardo da Vinci's Mona Lisa.

FLOUR POWER

Other people see a tortilla as a tasty snack, but Joe Bravo sees it as a canvas on which to create incredible works of art. The Los Angeles artist has earned such a reputation that some of his tortilla paintings sell for more than $3,000. Among those who have bought a Bravo creation is Flea, the bassist with the Red Hot Chili Peppers.

As an art student in the early 1970s, Bravo could not afford canvas, so he chose tortillas instead, reasoning that a staple Hispanic food was the ideal medium for displaying Hispanic imagery. He made a mobile of hanging tortillas—all hand-painted—but it blew apart in the Santa Ana winds. Then, nearly a decade ago, somebody reminded him about it and he started painting on tortillas again.

In his early days he used corn tortillas, but now he uses 26-in (66-cm) flour tortillas, custom-made by a Los Angeles company. He says: "An audience sees a painting on a little regular tortilla, they might go, 'OK.'

But to see a really, really big tortilla? That gets their attention."

His ideas are inspired by the individual texture, burn marks, and appearance of each toasted tortilla. He has re-created such diverse icons as Marilyn Monroe, Che Guevara, Ronald McDonald, and The Virgin of Guadalupe. For an exhibition in Hong Kong he chose Oriental themes, including dragons, pandas, and koi fish. He has also designed a tortilla mask and costume adorned with kernels of corn. "You're working with the environment of the tortilla," he explains. "The tortilla is almost like a collaborator."

"THE BRAVO CODE FOR TORTILLA PAINTING

Tortilla painting is more a collaboration between the artist and nature. It is not only about the artist painting on a tortilla, it is also about the tortilla suggesting themes for the artist to paint.

Visualize, contemplate, and imagine what the tortilla is conveying with its texture, burn marks, and appearance. Consider the tortilla as you would the smooth lines on a beautiful piece of natural wood, the veins of a marble stone, or the clouds in a bright blue sky. Use what you see on the tortilla as a starting point for your painting.

STEP 1: Let the tortilla dry either naturally (about 2–3 days) or in the oven (monitor carefully).

STEP 2: Cook the tortilla over an open flame on the stove top to get some interesting texture and color surfaces.

STEP 3: Varnish the tortilla on both sides, allowing each side to dry overnight.

STEP 4: Look at the tortilla and let it suggest something to you. Do you see people, a landscape, animals, stars, or other objects? Then paint what you see on the tortilla and have fun with it.

STEP 5: Once you finish painting, add several coats of varnish to the tortilla for further protection.

STEP 6: When dry, mount the tortilla in a shallow box frame or on some type of strong backing, such as a plastic plate, to display."

GUM ART

Street artists in London, England, use a variety of media to express themselves, including these paintings on discarded pieces of chewing gum. With an estimated 300,000 pieces of gum stuck to Oxford Street alone, the artists will never be short of materials.

TINY BOOK

Teeny Ted From Turnip Town, a book produced by the nanotechnology laboratory at Simon Frasier University, British Columbia, Canada, is so small that 20 copies of it can fit on the head a of a pin!

PAPER DRESSES

Thanks to Ed Livingston of Boston Harbor, Washington, women can read what they wear. That's because he makes women's dresses from newsprint!

POST-IT PORTRAIT

David Alvarez, 19, of Leavenworth, Washington, spent three months creating a three-dimensional portrait of Ray Charles that stood 10 ft (3 m) high from more than 2,000 colored Post-it® notes.

ALL CHANGE

It took six years for Mike and Annie Moore to cover every flat area in their McKittrick, California, bar with pennies—there were more than a million of them, glued to the walls, floors, ceiling, and furniture.

TONGUE TWISTER

A Chinese man has discovered that he can write with his tongue. Zhang Yongyang, of Xi'an City, found that he could touch his nose with his tongue and decided to use that dexterity in his hobby of calligraphy. So now he dips his tongue in ink and writes Chinese characters.

TRENDY TRASH

Justin Gignac has made trash trendy. He collects garbage from the streets of New York City, puts it in a box, labels it, and then sells it for up to $100!

COSTLY BLOW

Casino mogul Steve Wynn accidentally put his elbow through a Pablo Picasso painting shortly after he had agreed to sell it for a record $139 million. Wynn was showing the painting, called *Le Reve* ("The Dream"), to guests in his office at Las Vegas, Nevada, in 2006 when he caught the painting with his right elbow, causing a hole in the canvas the size of a silver dollar.

COBRA GUARD

In September 2007, Harrods Department Store in London, England, used live cobras to guard a $120,000 pair of shoes encrusted with diamonds, rubies, and sapphires.

HAIR DRESS

A model appeared on a catwalk in Zagreb, Croatia, in 2007 wearing a dress made entirely from human hair. Designers at the Artidjana company used 165 ft (50 m) of blonde hair in the dress.

LONG PAINTING

In 2007, some 3,500 people in Wakayama, Japan, combined their talents to create a painting that is 15,154 ft (4,663 m) long! It took them more than a month to complete.

DISNEY COLLECTION

In 2007, Disney unveiled a range of bridal dresses inspired by their fairytale films, including *Sleeping Beauty* and *Beauty and the Beast*. Created by L.A. designer Kirstie Kelly, the dresses cost from $1,500 each.

ART IN MOTION

In October 2006, German artist Carsten Hoeller installed five huge spiralling slides—the tallest being 180 ft (55 m) in height—as part of an exhibit at the art gallery Tate Modern in London, England.

COLOR-BLIND

Florida artist Jay Lonewolf Morales paints beautifully vivid pictures despite suffering from monochromacy—complete color blindness. He can see in only black and white and shades of gray, yet all his paintings are done with vibrant colors. He says: "I cry every time I paint, because I cannot enjoy the pigments of my labor."

TAB BELT

Sean Taylor of Stratford, New Jersey, has designed a belt—out of soda can tabs!

STOLEN KISS

Police charged a woman in Avignon, France, after she was caught kissing a $2-million painting by American abstract artist Cy Twombly. She was apparently so overcome with passion in front of the work that she just could not stop herself.

LONG SARI

A team of skilled weavers in India worked tirelessly for 14 days in 2007 to create a spectacular green-and-yellow sari that measured an amazing 2,226 ft (685 m) in length.

NAIL PAINTER

Instead of using a brush to create his paintings, Indian artist Nangaji Bhati simply grows his fingernails. By applying paint to the tip of his 4-in (10-cm) thumbnail, he is able to produce striking artworks on canvas.

Miniature Knitting

fine silk sewing thread, as well as needles made from stainless steel medical wire that is just 0.001 in (0.03 mm) thick. With this method she is able to create garments that have up to 80 stitches per inch.

It is not only the size of her "bug-knit" clothing that amazes people, but also the patterns on them. Her love of art has encouraged her to knit a tiny cardigan bearing a reproduction of a Picasso painting (right), a sweater with the design of an ancient Grecian urn, and a 2¼ x 1¼-in (5.7 x 3.2-cm) cardigan inspired by the treasures of King Tutankhamun's tomb. She has also knitted a pair of miniature "City-Country" socks—one sock featuring a pattern of the Chicago skyline, the other a country landscape—which sold for $750.

Since 2000, she has created countless items for dollhouse collectors and has had her work featured in the Radical Lace and Subversive Knitting exhibit at the Museum of Arts and Design in New York.

Of her miniature creations she says: "I really enjoy making clothes that don't have to fit and I love tricking the brain into thinking that things aren't miniature. Also, I don't spend a fortune on yarns—a little goes a long way."

Imagine a cardigan that is smaller than a dime—or a pair of gloves so tiny that a grain of rice would fit neatly into each finger. These, and other miniature marvels, are the creations of nano-knitter Althea Crome Merback.

Althea, from Bloomington, Indiana, knits cardigans, sweaters, and jackets on a 1:144 scale and gloves on a 1:12 scale by using

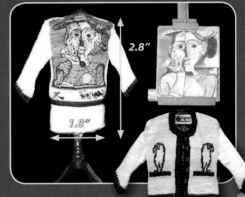

2.8"

1.8"

ACTUAL 1:1 SIZE!

"I believe that these tiny cardigans may be among the smallest cardigans in the world!"

"These City-Country socks represent my move from Chicago, Illinois, to Bloomington, Indiana."

"This sweater has the King of Hearts on one side and the Queen of Hearts on the other. The knitting's so fine that the sweaters are see-through!"

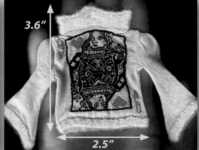

3.6"

2.5"

3.6"

2.5"

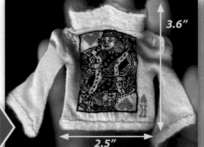

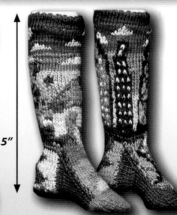

1.5"

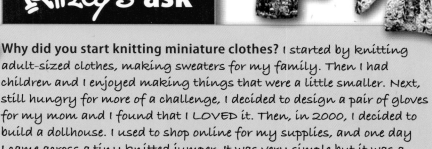

Ripley's ask

Why did you start knitting miniature clothes? I started by knitting adult-sized clothes, making sweaters for my family. Then I had children and I enjoyed making things that were a little smaller. Next, still hungry for more of a challenge, I decided to design a pair of gloves for my mom and I found that I LOVED it. Then, in 2000, I decided to build a dollhouse. I used to shop online for my supplies, and one day I came across a tiny knitted jumper. It was very simple but it was a lightbulb moment for me. I thought 'Hey, I bet I could do that.' So I found the smallest needles (probably a 0) and some baby yarn—it wasn't even that fine—and I knitted a man's cardigan that night. It was intoxicating and I was hooked from that point onward.

Do you use special knitting needles, and are they miniature? Yes, I have to make my own needles. I order 6-foot lengths of medical grade stainless steel, and cut and polish them to my desired length (usually 4, 5, or 6 inches long). They are very thin—some down to only 0.009 inches for the very tiniest sweaters. They are also very strong and have a high tensile strength so they can take a lot of bending and abuse without breaking.

What kind of wool do you use? I use mostly silk sewing threads—either 50 or 100 weight—but I have also used some very thin wools and cottons. I have a wool that isn't made any more that has about 25,000 feet to the pound so it is extremely thin.

How long does it take to knit a detailed miniature jumper? The longest it has ever taken was six months, the shortest was about six weeks.

Do you follow knitting patterns or do you make them up? I design all my own patterns. Usually I will have a vision of an image that I want to knit and then I will spend time designing the garment around that vision. I try to design everything with a very complete concept. For example, the ancient Greek sweater is shaped like a Greek vase, with a neck and foot and arms like a vase. The design elements on those parts of the sweater are designs found on Greek vases.

Can you explain what 'bug-knit' scale means? 'Bug-knit' scale simply means on a very small scale. However, most of the pieces I make are 1:12 scale which is a standard dollhouse scale. Some pieces are in 1:44 scale and on a very few occasions I have made 1:144 scale pieces.

What kind of reactions do you get to your work? Amazement. Really, people have been so generous with their praise and encouragement and it tickles me. I get so many emails from people just telling me 'Thank you for the eye candy.' I like that.

Is there anything you would like to knit that you haven't already? So much! I have a million ideas—I would like to knit a Roman relief, Japanese cranes, more artist-based sweaters like the Picasso and the Warhol. Hopefully my hands, eyes, and mind will hold out long enough to get just a fraction of them made.

2¼"

2¼"

"The front panels of my tiny Egyptian cardigan show the goddess Nut greeting King Tutankhamun; the back panel is an Egyptian amulet design."

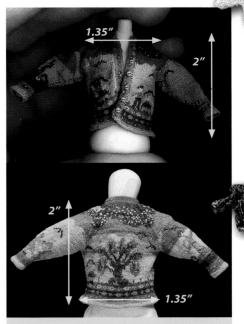

1.35"

2"

2"

1.35"

"The Earth to Sky cardigan takes the viewer on a journey extending deep into the earth's strata and far above the heavens—it's a cosmic landscape."

BRICK ART

Dubbed the Picasso of LEGO® bricks, Wall Street lawyer-turned-artist Nathan Sawaya creates astonishing masterpieces from the small building blocks beloved by children the world over. Requiring hours of painstaking work, each of his pieces can use more than 250,000 LEGO® bricks in total.

Sawaya was bestowed with the honor of becoming a Master Model Builder by LEGOLAND® California in 2004. The pieces shown here were displayed at Nathan's first solo art exhibition, The Art of the Brick, at the Lancaster Museum of Art in Philadelphia, Pennsylvania, in 2007.

Body

LEGO® SWIMMER

A giant plastic figure resembling a smiling LEGO® minifigure was fished out of the sea off the coast of Holland in August 2007. The 8-ft (2.4-m) model with a yellow head and blue body was found by workers in the Dutch resort of Zandvoort. Its origins were shrouded in mystery, but it was believed to have floated from the direction of England.

CHOCOLATE CHESS

An English artist has designed a chess set in which you can eat your opponent. Prudence Emma Staite from Gloucestershire, creates chocolate sculptures, and has made a chess set with playing pieces in white and milk chocolate arranged on a solid chocolate board. She also used more than 440 lb (200 kg) of Belgian chocolate to make a life-sized chocolate bed (complete with chocolate duvet and pillow) for England's Alton Towers theme park.

SIX FACES

A keen gardener has created replicas of the famous Moai statues on Easter Island in his hedge. Retired banker Michael Geiger used shears to clip six faces into the 12-ft (3.6-m) conifer hedge in his front garden in Billericay, England.

TOY CAR

An actual-size replica of a Volvo XC90 unveiled at the 2004 New York Auto Show was built from more than 200,000 LEGO® bricks. The car took a team of five builders two months to construct.

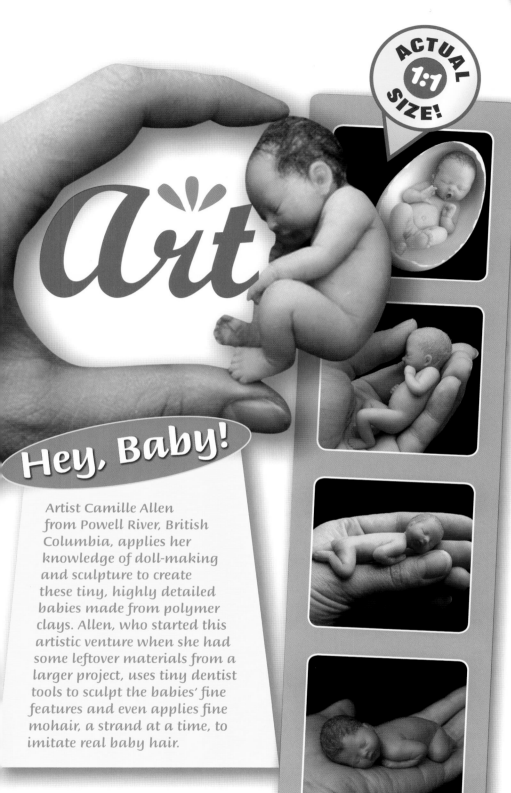

ACTUAL 1:1 SIZE!

Hey, Baby!

Artist Camille Allen from Powell River, British Columbia, applies her knowledge of doll-making and sculpture to create these tiny, highly detailed babies made from polymer clays. Allen, who started this artistic venture when she had some leftover materials from a larger project, uses tiny dentist tools to sculpt the babies' fine features and even applies fine mohair, a strand at a time, to imitate real baby hair.

TALL TOWER

In May 2007, visitors to LEGOLAND®, California, used 465,000 LEGO® bricks to build a tower an incredible 94 ft 4 in (28.7 m) tall.

SOIL TRIBUTE

Thousands of students from China's Zhongyuan University of Technology spent a day in March 2007 digging 96 faces out of the soil on the college campus to pay tribute to the country's farmers.

HEDGE MONSTER

John Dobson from Sussex, England, has spent 17 years creating a topiary model of the Loch Ness Monster in his garden hedge. He regularly trims the head, humps, and tail into the 15-ft-high (4.5-m) hedge. He is now growing another monster for his neighbor.

FAMOUS SCENES

Using the alias "Udronotto," Italian artist Marco Pece has re-created Leonardo da Vinci's painting of *The Last Supper* using LEGO® figures. He has also re-created the *Mona Lisa*, and movie scenes from *The Blues Brothers* and *The Graduate*.

POSTCARD CREATIONS

British artist David Mach creates works of art from postcards. In 2007, he used 8,000 identical postcards of Dubai's Jumeirah Emirates Towers to create a picture of a racehorse that measured 12 x 9 ft (3.6 x 2.7 m).

STILL LIFE

Discovering that his former hometown of Teococuilco, Mexico, had turned into a ghost town over the past 30 years, sculptor Alejandro Santiago decided to repopulate the area with 2,501 clay statues.

DISTINCTIVE DESK

Designer Eric Harshbarger has built a full-sized office desk from 35,000 LEGO® bricks for a company in Seattle. The desk weighs around 120 lb (55 kg) and has seven working drawers. After creating the prototype, he had to take it apart and then glue each piece back together to make the desk stronger.

SCULPTURE RISES

A prolonged drought in Utah's Great Salt Lake resulted in a sculpture that had been buried for over 30 years suddenly emerging above the surface. In 1970, artist Robert Smithson used 6,650 tons of black basalt and earth to create "Spiral Jetty," a structure measuring 1,500 ft (460 m) in length that coiled around in the water. For three decades it was visible only from the air until lack of rainfall exposed it to a wider audience.

WOOLEN HOUSE

Five-hundred women from across the world—including the United States, Canada, and Europe—knitted for thousands of hours to create a 140-sq-ft (13-sq-m) woolen house. The brainchild of British knitter Alison Murray, the multi-colored "Gingerbread House," displayed in Devon, England, in 2007, was made from millions of stitches. It had 1,000 knitted roof tiles and was surrounded by a knitted garden, with knitted flowers and knitted trees 12 ft (3.6 m) tall.

CAR-TOON TRUCK

New Jersey art teacher Robert Luczun has decorated every inch of a 1928 Model AR Ford Roadster pickup truck with hundreds of comic book, comic strip, and animated cartoon characters.

Combining his twin hobbies of antique cars and comic art, he spent more than 2,800 hours over a period of 15 months airbrush-painting assorted animated icons, from 101 Dalmatians to Rat Fink and Finding Nemo to Dr. Who. The result is a rolling history of comics from 1896 to the present day.

After months of preparation, Luczun waited another three days so that he could start painting on October 18, 2004—the 108th anniversary of the first published comic, *The Yellow Kid*, whom he honored with a place on the back of the side mirror.

Each cartoon was hand-drawn twice—once on a paper layout, then again on the vehicle—and every color was masked off to prevent any spray-paint errors. He took much of the truck apart during the project. The desire to cover the entire bodywork—inside and out—forced him to paint in backbreaking positions. While drawing, he put the Where's Waldo? figure in at random and finished up with around a dozen Waldos scattered about the vehicle. Luczun's incredible cartoon truck is now a familiar sight at comic book conventions, auto shows, and art car parades.

The interior of the tailgate of Robert's car features a Ripley's Believe It or Not! cartoon (left).

14

The gas tank is located on the front of the windshield and has a mix of characters from Harvey, Merrie Melodies, and Warner Bros. This area was drawn and painted directly on to the truck— hanging over it!

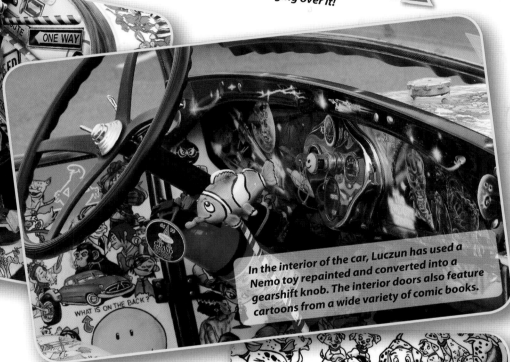

In the interior of the car, Luczun has used a Nemo toy repainted and converted into a gearshift knob. The interior doors also feature cartoons from a wide variety of comic books.

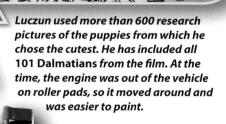

Luczun used more than 600 research pictures of the puppies from which he chose the cutest. He has included all 101 Dalmatians from the film. At the time, the engine was out of the vehicle on roller pads, so it moved around and was easier to paint.

In Luczun's own words...

"Other airbrush artists look at me as if I'm nuts when they see the truck and what it took to get there. At least I don't have any worry about anyone trying to copy it!

My thoughts while working on each cartoon were that this was someone's favorite and this was the only one they were looking for, so it had to be perfect. One lady started hitting her husband when she saw a comic, saying: "That's the one I was talking about all these years!" Another time I had to remove the rear license plate so that a chap could get a few pictures of a cartoon—that was to be his next tattoo.

For '101 Dalmatians,' I must have collected 600 puppy pictures and I chose the cutest ones. I checked off each picture as I completed it, but just when I thought I'd finished, a piece of paper flew to the floor. It was two puppies that didn't have a check mark. So I went back and put a piece of tape on each one as I counted... 99. I put the last two in, and yes, I do have 101!

The idea to have a fun vehicle that everyone could relate to got bigger than I ever dreamed. It took on a life of its own. Some of the original cartoon artists have contributed new drawings, on 3 x 4-in plates, that I have fixed to the floor of the truck's bed. They all want to be part of what they call a comic icon.

I think the best part is the joy I get when a person says to me, 'I never thought I'd see that cartoon ever again, it was my favorite. Thanks for letting me re-live a fun part of my life!'"

During an art exhibition in Norway, artist Jan Christensen had his work, *Relative Value*, made out of 100,000 kroner ($16,300) worth of bank notes, stolen out of its frame by bandits in a gallery robbery.

Eighteen hundred people, ranging from two-year-old children to senior citizens, created a 20,000-sq-ft (1,858-sq-m) finger painting in just one day at New Paltz, New York, in September 2007.

Art students in China have been painting live pigs to create colorful images as the animals roam in a field. The students from Sichuan Fine Arts Institute chose pigs because they represent harmony and happiness.

CRAYON SCULPTURE

No school bag ever housed a set of crayons like these, but U.S. sculptor Pete Goldlust has turned art on its head by carving intricate designs into ordinary wax crayons.

NAKED SHOOT

More than 600 naked people were photographed as a living sculpture on a Swiss glacier in 2007. The photo shoot was arranged by New York artist Spencer Tunick to raise awareness of the effect of climate change on shrinking Swiss glaciers.

FRIDGEHENGE FALLS

In Santa Fe, New Mexico, artist Adam Horowitz created a replica of Stonehenge from more than 100 old refrigerators. The refrigerators, stacked and arranged in a ring like the famous English landmark, became a popular tourist attraction. They stood for nearly a decade until, in 2007, the 80-ft (24-m) structure was demolished by a mixture of high winds and the city council.

FACE-PAINTERS

In June 2006, a team of five face-painters painted a total of 989 faces in four hours at Longleat House, Wiltshire, England.

DORMANT TALENT

Sleepwalker Lee Hadwin of Henllan, North Wales, is a talented artist when he is asleep— but when awake he struggles to draw at all! Wandering around the house in his sleep, he draws anywhere—even on walls and tables—but experts are baffled as to why he cannot re-create these works of art when he wakes up.

FIELD ART

In a clover field at the Thomas Bull Memorial Park in New York, artist Roger Baker mowed an image of a Purple Heart medal, which is given to U.S. servicemen who are killed or wounded in action, that measured an astonishing 850,000 sq ft (79,000 sq m).

SPILT MILK

An artist from Devon, England, did not cry over 1,300 gal (5,000 l) of spilled milk. Instead, Martin White poured it into a huge dish, 30 ft (9 m) in diameter, and left it to turn sour as a work of art. Entitled *Spilt Milk*, it was designed to highlight the pressures faced by dairy farmers.

SCRABBLE® BLING

Boise, Idaho, artist Millie Hilgert creates jewelry from discarded items. Vinyl records are made into necklaces, earrings, and rings; game pieces from dominoes or Scrabble® are converted into bracelets; bottle caps are turned into necklaces; and jar lids become belt buckles.

CHOC STAR

In 2005, Madame Tussauds created a life-size model of musical supremo Sir Elton John—in chocolate. Made to the singer's measurements, it was built from 227 lb (103 kg) of chocolate and took more than 1,000 hours to create. The finished product was displayed at the London, England, tourist attraction in a special air-conditioned tent to stop it from melting.

OLD HEART

Jennifer Sutton was able to view a unique exhibit at an art gallery in London, England, in 2007—her old heart! The 23-year-old science graduate from Hampshire had her diseased heart removed in a transplant operation earlier in the year and agreed to allow it to be displayed in a jar as part of an exhibition that explored the historical significance of the human heart in art, literature, and medicine.

DUAL PURPOSE

Gala Contemplating the Mediterranean Sea Which at Twenty Meters Becomes a Portrait of Abraham Lincoln, painted by Spanish artist Salvador Dali in 1976, is both a painting of his wife and a pixilated portrait of U.S. President Abraham Lincoln!

R.A.P. ARTIST

Portuguese artist Leonel Moura has built a Robotic Action Painter—a robot that creates its own art. He has also constructed "the first zoo for artificial life," filled with 45 robots (each representing a different creature) housed in cages and enclosures.

RELIGIOUS SIGN?

Visitors flocked to the home of Eric Nathaniel in Port Blair, Andaman Islands, India, in 2007, after two of his paintings of Jesus began to drip red fluid. Experts suggested it was more likely to be red paint from the pictures melting in the humidity, than blood.

ICE QUEEN

In 2007, sculptors Ivo Piazza and Rainer Kasslatter created a huge sculpture of Marilyn Monroe—from ice. It earned them first prize at an annual ice-sculpture contest in Austria.

BRICK DRAGON

A model dragon at the LEGOLAND® Windsor theme park in England has been built from nearly one million LEGO® bricks. The "Ice Dragon" measures 30 ft (9 m) in length, weighs nearly 3 tons, and took 2,200 hours to build. It is so big that it had to be built in nine sections before being hoisted into place.

Crystal Curiosities

Dutch artist Hans van Bentem makes beautiful crystal chandeliers in the most amazing, avant-garde designs—ranging from a champagne bottle to a skull and crossbones. Abandoning the traditional chandelier shape, he has also created chandeliers in the design of a globe, a spider, an easel and brushes, a heraldic lion, a fighter plane, a seahorse, a violin, a pipe, and even a gun. He says he finds his inspiration in art history, comic strips, and the world of modern communication. Each piece takes up to two months to create and sells from $16,000.

SHAKESPEARE RECITAL

In February 2004, more than 150 members of the Wellesley College, Massachusetts, Shakespeare Society read aloud the complete works of Shakespeare (a total of 39 plays, 154 sonnets and poetry) in 22 hours 5 minutes.

LATE RETURN

Robert Nuranen of Hancock, Michigan, paid $171 in late fees when he returned a library book 47 years after he had borrowed it.

Ripley's research........................

The Last Supper took Mark Beekman a year to make. He began by buying up all the Lite-Brite pegs he could find—both direct from the manufacturer Hasbro and local suppliers—and constructing a frame out of lightweight aluminum pipes. He used perforated sheet metal as backing and employed computer printouts of the original painting to help him work out where the different-colored plastic pegs should go. The pegs were then attached to the metal backing with eight layers of glue. He painted the frame antique gold and backlit his creation with high-tech electroluminescent panels.

LITE SUPPER

Artist Mark Beekman from Charlestown, Pennsylvania, used more than 125,000 Lite-Brite pegs to create a 1:9-scale version of Leonardo da Vinci's painting *The Last Supper* that measured 5 ft (1.5 m) tall by 10 ft (3 m) wide.

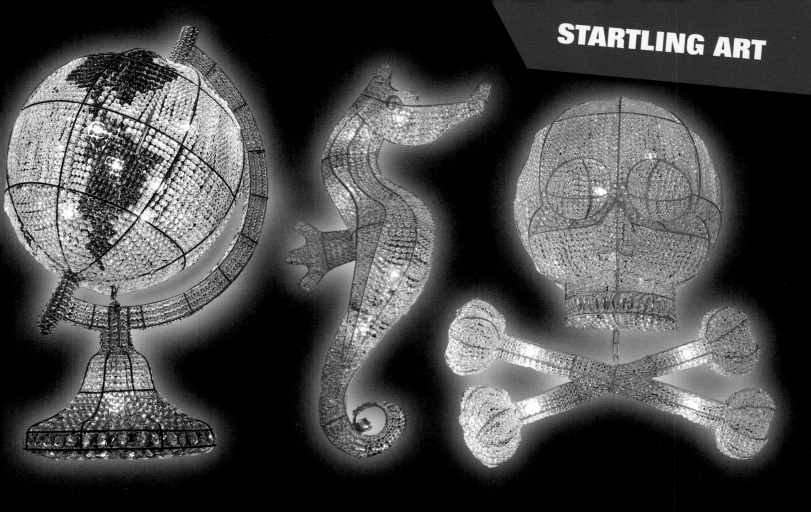

PROLIFIC AUTHOR
At her most prolific, British romantic author Barbara Cartland completed a novel every two weeks. Altogether, she published 723 novels in her 70-year career!

TINY SUN
Using a new nanoprinting technique, Swiss computer experts have created an image of the Sun that is just 80 microns wide—less than one-tenth the size of a pinhead!

GUITAR GATHERING
In June 2007, Kansas City radio station KYYS (99.7FM) assembled a ballpark full of 1,721 guitarists—ages ranging from five to 60—to play Deep Purple's song "Smoke on the Water" simultaneously.

TOP BRASS
A band of German musicians staged a concert on a Bolivian mountain top in 2007. They played instruments at the summit of the Acotango Volcano for 30 minutes at an altitude of 19,855 ft (6,052 m).

BABOON'S BUTT
Matthew Roby from Lancashire, England, creates characters from old bits of machinery and scrap metal. Nothing goes to waste—he even used the bright orange ballcocks from a toilet system for a baboon's butt!

ONE-NOTE GIG
The White Stripes finished their 2007 Canadian tour by playing a show just one note long. Jack and Meg White took to the stage in St. John's, Newfoundland, played a C-sharp accompanied by a bang of the cymbals, announced that they had now officially played in every province and territory in Canada, and left the stage. Fans had been warned that the show would be just one note long, but still hundreds turned up. Later, the band played a full-length set elsewhere in the city. Previous venues on their quirky tour had included a bowling alley in Saskatoon and a Winnipeg Transit bus.

YODEL-AY!
More than 1,000 American yodelers converge on Salt Lake City, Utah, each June for the Swiss Singing and Yodeling Festival.

CURTAIN CALLS
Italian opera star Luciano Pavarotti, who died in 2007, once received an astonishing 165 curtain calls at the end of a stage show.

WOODEN HORSE
Saimir Strati of Albania, has created a mosaic of a leaping horse that is 13 ft (4 m) long—from more than half a million toothpicks. It took him 40 days to construct, working 13 hours a day.

TINY SCISSORS
In 2003, Chen Yu Pei of China, designed a pair of stainless steel scissors that measured just 0.068 in (1.75 mm) long and 0.054 in (1.38 mm) wide—and they actually worked!

SLEEPING STATUE
A 1,365-ft-long (415-m) sleeping Buddha statue has been carved into the side of a mountain in Yiyang, Jiangxi, China.

INSURED EYES
Cross-eyed silent movie star Ben Turpin was insured for $500,000 against the possibility of his eyes ever becoming normal again.

ROOT CARVER
Micro-artist Shelvaraj from Nagapattinam, India, carves tiny ornate figures from the roots of trees. Shelvaraj, who has been pursuing his art since his teens, specializes in religious figures and has carved a row of elephants, ranging in size from a minute speck to $3/8$ in (1 cm) tall.

COCONUT ORCHESTRA
The cast and creators of the Monty Python musical *Spamalot* led 5,567 people in a mass coconut orchestra as they clip-clopped in time to "Always Look on the Bright Side of Life" in Trafalgar Square in London, England, in April 2007.

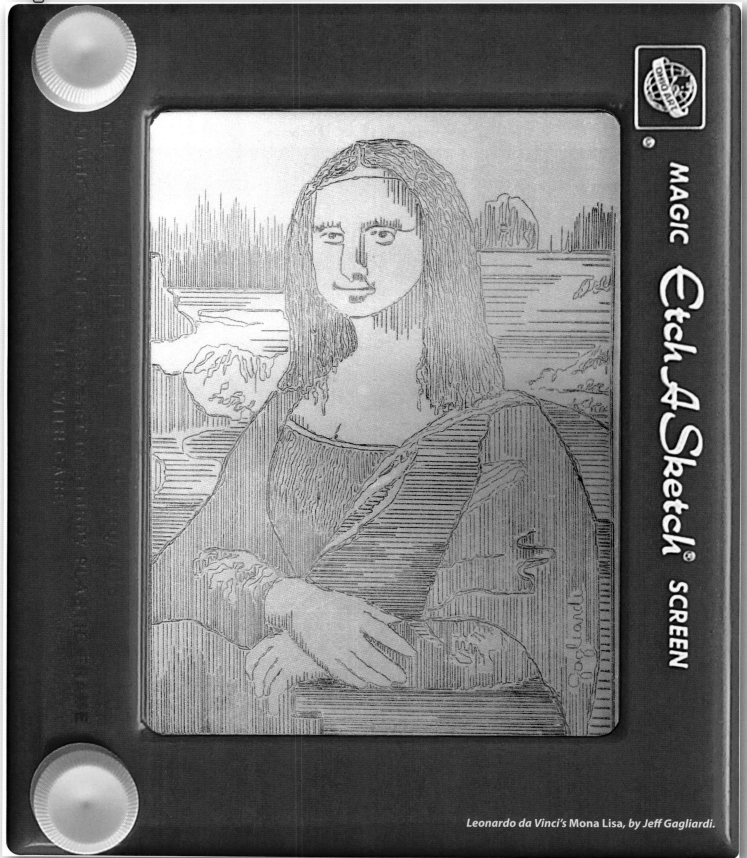

MAGIC Etch A Sketch® SCREEN

Leonardo da Vinci's Mona Lisa, by Jeff Gagliardi.

Some artists work in oils, others choose watercolors, but Jeff Gagliardi of Boulder, Colorado, prefers a different artistic medium—the Etch A Sketch® drawing toy. Using this much-loved children's toy of the 1960s, Gagliardi has been able to create wonderful works of art. He has had exhibitions at some of the United States' leading galleries and his Etch A Sketch® version of Leonardo da Vinci's *Mona Lisa* has been valued at $10,000!

Amazingly, Gagliardi never had an Etch A Sketch® as a child but developed an interest while playing with his nephew's. He first tried it out seriously while at art college in New York in the early 1970s. He says: "I did a drawing of the Taj Mahal, complete with reflecting pools. Quite frankly, I didn't think it was a big deal, but my family wouldn't let me erase it. From that point on it became apparent that I had some sort of gift for drawing on this little toy. People would walk past the serious work I was doing as a painter and want to see the Etch A Sketch® drawings."

Ripley's ask

How do you create your works of art? Each sketch takes a lot of planning as to how I'll start and where I'll end, but I also need to plan how to interpret a painted piece into a line drawing—how to render the subtle shading, for example.

How long does it take? Because each piece is only one unbroken line, much of the work is in retracing lines to get back and forth between areas. Also, in the case of the 'Mona Lisa,' I do what I think will be the most difficult areas first (her face and smile) and then I do the rest. Typically, this can take from five to 20 hours—in the case of 'Mona Lisa,' closer to 20.

Which is your favorite? I like 'Mona Lisa' the best. Partly because of her sweetly subtle smile and the fact that she's drawn sidewise in order to get her in portrait mode. I am also very fond of my 'Vitruvian Man' tribute, as it is done with an economy of lines (true to da Vinci's style!).

Vincent van Gogh's Starry Night, *in* Etch A Sketch®.

Since then he has re-created details from Michelangelo's Sistine Chapel and copied paintings by Van Gogh.

His work requires enormous patience. Pictures are drawn by twiddling two knobs, which operate a stylus across the underside of the glass, scraping a line in the aluminum coating. The toy's system operates horizontally, which means that to create a vertical portrait—as in the Mona Lisa—Gagliardi has to draw sidewise!

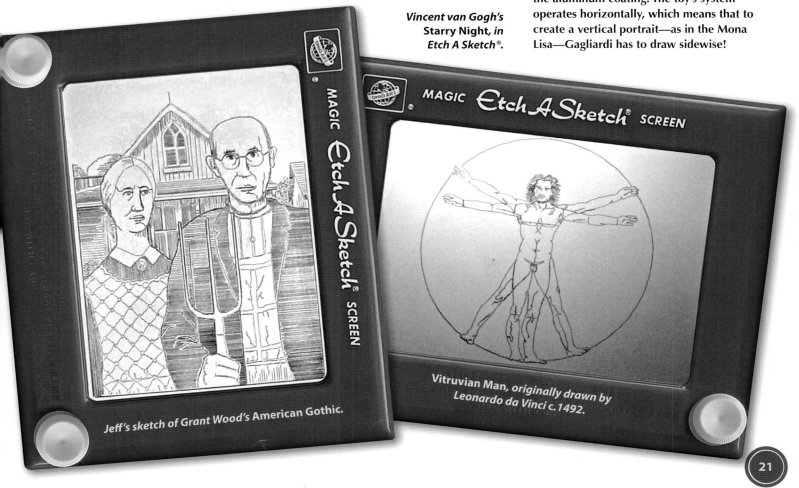

Jeff's sketch of Grant Wood's American Gothic.

Vitruvian Man, *originally drawn by* Leonardo da Vinci c. 1492.

Enter the Vault

PEN-KNIFE SCULPTURE ▶

Displaying 1,936 blades in 1936, the "Year Knife" was the creation of cutlery makers Joseph Rodgers & Sons of Sheffield, England. The company started assembling their creation in 1822, with 1,822 blades, and added a new blade every year thereafter.

BOTTLE CAP INN

The Bottle Cap Inn was the appropriate name for this bar in Miami, Florida, that was decorated with more than 300,000 bottle caps in the 1930s.

ROBERT RIPLEY

Seen here in the 1940s drawing one of his famous cartoons, Robert Ripley used to receive thousands of letters from devoted fans every week, all hoping to have their unbelievable facts included in his cartoon strip.

◀ LINE ART

The famous portrait of George Washington that graces the front of every $1 bill and Emanual Leutze's well-known painting, "Washington Crossing the Delaware," are both re-created here in a 1932 drawing by Forest Ages McGinn—drawn in a single continuous line without lifting the pencil from the page!

CARTOON CAPERS

Clarence Thorpe of Riverside, California, could simultaneously draw cartoons with his hands and feet. Thorpe first appeared at Ripley's Dallas Odditorium in 1936.

BELIEVE ◀ IT OR NOT! BLOUSES

Blouses featuring Ripley's Believe It or Not! cartoons were sold at the Ripley's New York City Odditorium in 1939. During the 1930s, the worldwide-syndicated Ripley cartoons had more than 80 million readers daily.

BLIND SCULPTOR

Mark Shoesmith of New York, seen here with his model, sculpted this bust of Robert Ripley in 1938. Remarkably, Shoesmith was blind and achieved Ripley's likeness purely by touching his face.

BIBLICAL ART

This drawing of a praying child is made entirely from the words of the New Testament. It was created by Korean artist Gwang Hyuk Rhee in the 1950s.

COMPUTER CASTLE

A teacher from Shandong Industrial Arts College, China, created a sculpture of a castle from the parts of an old computer. The piece, titled *Fossil*, was exhibited at Shandong Museum in 2007.

BARGAIN BUY

Michael Sparks of Nashville, Tennessee, bought a 184-year-old print of the American Declaration of Independence for $2.48 at a thrift store. Appraisers estimate that it is worth at least 100,000 times that price!

LONG OVERDUE

In 1650, the Bishop of Winchester, England, borrowed a book from Somerset County Records office but it was not returned to Somerset County Library until 1985—335 years later—by which time it had accrued $6,000 in unpaid fees. The title of the overdue book? *The Book of Fines*!

TXT BK

The Last Messages, a novel by Hannu Luntiala of Finland, consists exclusively of text messages exchanged between the main character and his friends and relatives.

SENIOR SINGERS

A new band made an assault on the U.K. and U.S. charts in 2007—even though they had a combined age of more than 3,000 years! The Zimmers were a group of 40 British seniors who became a surprise Internet hit with their version of The Who's "My Generation," complete with its inappropriate line "I hope I die before I get old."

SKIN BINDING

A 300-year-old book discovered in the center of Leeds, Yorkshire, England, in 2006 is thought to have been bound in human skin. The book was written mainly in French and was published at a time when accounts of murder trials were sometimes bound in the killer's skin.

ODD TITLES

A book titled *The Stray Shopping Carts of Eastern North America: A Guide to Field Identification* was named the oddest book title for 2007 in an annual competition. Its author, Julian Montague, beat off stiff competition from *Tattooed Mountain Women and Spoon Boxes of Dagestan*, *How Green Were the Nazis?*, and *Better Never to Have Been: The Harm of Coming Into Existence*.

BIKE LINE

Rod Pasold of Blue River, Wisconsin, has created a work of art consisting of a line of 30 old motorcycles chained to posts and adorned by approximately 200 different colored crash helmets. To give the bikes a distinctive look, many of them have been customized with add-ons, such as a set of antlers and an animal skull.

HARD FRIES

British sculptor Keith Tyson made models of every item on a KFC menu, even down to the fries—in lead. His other weird and wonderful works have included pouring a thimble full of paint from a skyscraper and attaching 366 chopping boards to a wall.

SAND TEMPLE

Indian sculptor Sudarsan Patnaik created a lifelike replica of the Taj Mahal—in sand. It took him 56 working hours to complete the model, which stood 15 ft (4.5 m) high.

STAMP PORTRAITS

Artist Pete Mason, from Hednesford, Staffordshire, England, creates amazing portraits of famous people from thousands of used postage stamps. He sketches each portrait on to a grid before painstakingly cutting the individual stamps to size and sticking them in place. In 2007, he completed a 12,000-stamp tribute to Princess Diana, which measured 7 x 7 ft (2.1 x 2.1 m), to mark the tenth anniversary of her death. His previous works have included prime ministers Winston Churchill and Tony Blair, soccer star David Beckham, and Queen Elizabeth II.

MANILOW SENTENCE

People who break the noise laws in Fort Lupton, Colorado, are given an unusual sentence—they are forced to listen to Barry Manilow music for an hour! The punishment is the idea of Judge Paul Sacco, who claims that offenders who go through the Manilow treatment rarely re-offend. Also on his punishment playlist are The Carpenters, Dolly Parton, and Barney the Dinosaur.

BABY BOOMERANG

In 1997, Sadir Kattan of Australia, created a boomerang smaller than the palm of his hand that could be thrown 65½ ft (20 m) and returned accurately.

HAIR SCULPTURE

For a 2007 exhibition, Chinese artist Wenda Gu created a sculpture using more than 7 mi (11 km) of braided human hair.

SMALL IS BEAUTIFUL

A pinhead-sized replica of the Lloyd's of London building sold for $180,000 at an auction in 2007. The model, which was an exact replica of the famous building, took English micro-sculptor Willard Wigan four months to create, using white gold and platinum. The sculpture can be viewed only through a microscope. Wigan, whose previous works include re-creating the Statue of Liberty inside the eye of a needle, said that the Lloyd's of London building was the most difficult piece he has ever made.

OUTSIZE ALBUM

A photo album unveiled in Orlando, Florida, in 2007 was so big that it needed two adults to turn each of its 20 pages. Created for the launch of the 2008 Dodge Grand Caravan, it measured 9 ft (3 m) wide by 12 ft (4 m) tall.

Disk Dragon

Sculptors in China built a huge dragon-shaped lamp from hundreds of used computer disks for a 2007 carnival at Beijing International Sculpture Park.

SMALL WORLD

Mysterious tiny figures have been appearing all over the city of London, England. They are the work of British artist Slinkachu, who has been painting the small plastic people used in architects' models and planting them in streets and on benches across the capital. His "Little People" were inspired by the idea of a hidden world existing right in front of our eyes.

NO VERBS

In 2004, a French author writing under the pseudonym Michel Thaler wrote a 233-page novel, *Le Train de Nulle Part*, without the use of a single verb.

SCRAP ELEPHANTS

Jim Powers of Gage, Oklahoma, has created giant insects, life-size elephants, and dinosaurs out of scrap metal from cars.

TOOTHPICK MODELS

Chicago, Illinois, artist Wayne Kusy spent eight years building a 25-ft-long (7.5-m) model of the ocean liner *Queen Mary* from 814,000 toothpicks. A specialist in toothpick ships, he has also made replicas of the English tea clipper *Cutty Sark*, and the ill-fated liners *Titanic* and *Lusitania*.

TWISTED TREES

The tree circus of Gilroy Gardens features one-of-a-kind tree sculptures—with various grafts, twists, and bends—all grown over 30 years by a farmer in California.

SKEWER CITY

Edgar Gata of Las Pinas City, Philippines, used more than 30,000 wooden barbecue skewers to assemble a model town with dozens of buildings, vehicles, and landmarks from around the world.

THE SMALL TOP

Sculpting nearly 400 characters from clay, Sonny King of Los Angeles, California, has created a miniature circus. Each diorama took three months to make, and the model is based on his father Mervyn's adventures as a circus-owner in the 1940s and 1950s. Models include his father in the lion's cage, and veteran strong man Johnny Zelinsky, who could hold aloft a trapeze artist using only his teeth when he was in his eighties!

LONG NOTE

In September 2007, saxophonist Aaron Bing of Jacksonville, Florida, held a single, continuous low G note on his saxophone for 39 minutes 40 seconds while standing on a windy New York City street.

GUN PLAY

Colombian musician and anti-violence advocate Cesar Lopez creates and plays guitars built from guns.

THE HILLS ARE ALIVE

The city of Salzburg, Austria, has a cable channel that plays the movie *The Sound of Music* 24 hours a day, every day of the year!

CYMBAL OF COURAGE

Despite being born without lower arms and a badly deformed leg, which was later amputated, 15-year-old Cornel Hrisca-Munn of Whittington, England, beat 420 able-bodied youngsters to take second place in a national drumming competition. He uses straps to attach the drumsticks to his upper arms and a false leg so that he can operate the bass pedal.

CHAMBER MUSIC

Police in Bolzano, Italy, seized a toilet from an art gallery because it played Italy's national anthem while flushing.

NONSTOP ELVIS

Elvis impersonator Gaétan Lalonde of St.-Jérôme, Quebec, Canada, sang numbers by the King nonstop for two days in June 2007. The singer, also known as Scotty Davis, performed a rotation of 44 tunes over the course of 46 hours 30 minutes.

KERMIT FAN

A 21-year-old man claiming to have a bomb took over a radio station in Wanganui, New Zealand, in 1995 and demanded to hear the song "Rainbow Connection" by Kermit the Frog played non-stop for 12 hours!

BURSTING WITH PRIDE

Canadian artist Sean Rooney makes amazing sculptures from balloons—flowers, creatures, even costumes. In June 2007, he built a 20-ft (6-m) pyramid sculpture out of hundreds of balloons for a children's festival in Sarajevo, Bosnia.

MIXED MESSAGE

Mourners at a funeral service in Kent, England, were startled when the church PA system accidentally played Rod Stewart's 1978 hit "Do Ya Think I'm Sexy," which includes the inappropriate line "If you want my body... "!

PLASTIC FANTASTIC

Luis Torres, a Metropolitan Transit Authority worker who lives in New York City, crafts sculptures from the transit credit cards that he collects during his day-job.

EXTRA LARGE

It took Wu Shujun of Handan, China, nearly four years to make this sweater—not surprising as it is 16 ft (5 m) long, 8 ft (2.5 m) high and weighs 22 lb (10 kg). The logo on the front of the sweater was designed to herald the 2008 Beijing Olympics.

STONE COOKIES

Artist Robin Antar from Brooklyn, New York, can create everyday objects from stone. Even though Robin is blind in one eye, she carves lifelike stone sculptures of iconic American items, such as a pair of Diesel jeans, a bag of Milano cookies, a Skechers' logger boot, a bag of M&M's®, and a giant Heinz Ketchup bottle. She usually works on her sculptures at night and spends up to six months on each piece. Her sculptures are so realistic that they have to be roped off to stop exhibit visitors trying to help themselves to a stone cookie or an M&M®!

PRIZE PUMPKINS

Like thousands of American youngsters, Scott Cummins used to carve out a pumpkin to make a jack-o-lantern for Halloween. But whereas others mastered just the basic eyes, nose, and mouth, Cummins has gone on to create amazingly intricate works of art from the fruit.

The junior high school teacher from Perryton, Texas, has been carving pumpkins since he was 16. His extensive portfolio includes portraits of Leonard Nimoy, Albert Einstein, and George W. Bush; characters such as Gollum from *The Lord of the Rings* and Winnie-the-Pooh; lifelike animal heads; expressive faces born of his own imagination; the Statue of Liberty; and a beautiful baby in the womb. Each carving takes him just a couple of hours.

Sometimes the shape of the pumpkin dictates the face; at other times he has an idea of what he wants to create and looks for a pumpkin of appropriate form and size. He begins by scraping away the inside of the pumpkin and the tough orange skin. For the actual carving, he uses a variety of implements—sharpened spoons, ice-cream scoops, knives, drill bits, and even saw blades—and is always on the lookout for new tools.

Finally, he lights many of the carved pumpkins with a 30-watt bulb, and, as the light shines through the thinner areas of the rind, his fantastic creations acquire an eerie, almost mystical appearance.

Ripley's ask

" How do you choose what to sculpt and do you take requests? I just find myself overcome with the feeling that some particular character or expression really NEEDS to be captured in pumpkin rind. The shape of the pumpkin also affects my decision. I take "suggestions" once in a while. Not too many requests though.

What is your favorite and why? I don't really have a favorite. I guess I can say that I'm very fond of the Albert Einstein carving... probably because the image is so iconic.

How long does each sculpture take? Eleven months of planning and anticipation and about an hour or two of actual carving.

To date, what is your total number of pumpkin carvings? I'd say about a wagon load. Somewhere over one hundred, I suppose. Since I began photographing them, most are on my online gallery.

Do you like pumpkin pie? It's delicious.

What do you do with the pumpkins once you have finished carving? I display them, take a picture or two, and then I allow them to decompose with quiet dignity.

What will you do next? I'll probably keep on carving. I'd like to do more Tiki faces and maybe a zombie or two. Or I could retire to an exotic location and get fat off the enormous wealth from my pumpkin-carving empire! "

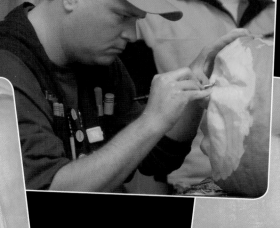

Scott breathes life into his pumpkins using a selection of instruments and his considerable carving skills.

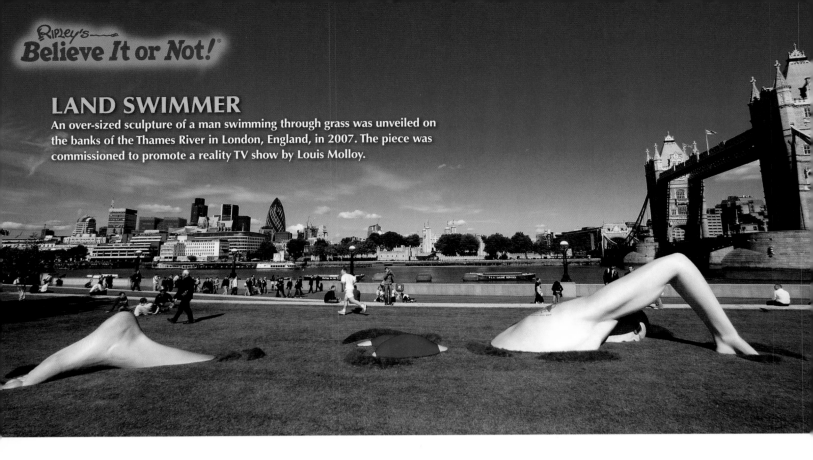

LAND SWIMMER

An over-sized sculpture of a man swimming through grass was unveiled on the banks of the Thames River in London, England, in 2007. The piece was commissioned to promote a reality TV show by Louis Molloy.

FIREARM ART

Peace art project artists in Cambodia created original sculptures and furniture from decommissioned pistols and assault rifles.

TIN PANTS

A pair of jeans 16 ft (5 m) tall made from 3,000 soft drinks cans was on display at a shopping mall in Xiamen City, China, in October 2007.

TAPING DAVE

Judy Carter of Seymour, Indiana, created a sculpture of TV host David Letterman using duct tape!

FILMED FLIGHT

In 2005, Francisco Gutierrez flew with a swarm of Monarch butterflies to film the flight of their 4,375-mi (7,040 km) migration from Canada to Mexico. Gutierrez flew among the thousands of insects in a small ultralight plane.

TRASH PEOPLE

A thousand trash people—molded from tin cans, computer parts, and crushed plastic—have appeared in some of the world's most famous locations. The work of German artist H.A. Schult, the garbage army has been arranged on the Great Wall of China, near the Egyptian Pyramids, in Moscow's Red Square, at the base of the Matterhorn mountain in Switzerland, and in front of Cologne Cathedral in Germany.

HOMEMADE BANJO

Dean Clemmer of Bolivar, Missouri, has been in a band since 1999 playing a five-string banjo made from a car's hubcap!

TV GLUT

The average U.S. home has more television sets than it has people, and believe it or not, one in four Americans have actually appeared on TV!

GAME HOST

A Swedish TV presenter became a hit on the Internet site YouTube after she vomited live on air. Eva Nazemson was hosting a late-night phone-in game show when she suddenly felt ill. As a caller tried to solve a puzzle, she quickly turned her head to one side and vomited before bravely carrying on with the program.

BURNING AMBITION

In June 2006, a man from Beijing, China, fled a burning house with only his television set... which he immediately plugged in elsewhere so that he could continue to watch a World Cup soccer match!

EDIBLE MOZART

Japan's Junko Terashima prepared an amazing likeness of the composer Wolfgang Amadeus Mozart—from food! Terashima is an expert in Bento Art—the Japanese craft of lunch sculpture—whereby incredible edible images are created from fruit, vegetables, and other foodstuffs.

TITANIC TIME

Watchmaker Romain Jerome of Geneva, Switzerland, has created a line of watches that use steel and coal that has been taken from the wreck of the R.M.S. Titanic. Incorporating steel from the stricken ship's hull and coal from the wreck site, the watches sell for anything between $8,000 and $175,000.

OPTICAL ILLUSION

American street artist Kurt Wenner adds the finishing touches to a 3-D work of art at Waterloo Station in London, England. The classically inspired Wenner has pioneered an art form known as anamorphic, in which a street painting creates an optical illusion by popping up in 3-D when viewed from a certain angle. Here he appears to sit obliviously on a sofa while a taxi crashes through the walls of the house.

CARDBOARD CARS

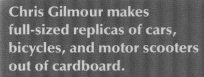

Chris Gilmour makes full-sized replicas of cars, bicycles, and motor scooters out of cardboard.

Using nothing more than cardboard and glue—and with no supporting wood or metal framework—the English-born artist creates amazingly lifelike models. His "Pussy Galore" car, exhibited in New York in 2006, is an exact replica of James Bond's famous Aston Martin, right down to tire-slashers, machine guns, and rocket launchers. Although made of cardboard, it is valued at $30,000.

Gilmour uses cardboard partly because it is so easy to find—he collects discarded pieces from dumpsters near his base in Udine, Italy. Sometimes he even leaves the original printing, tape, and labels on to emphasize the fact that he is creating coveted items from what is merely waste material.

His first big piece was a cardboard cow and he has since created such diverse everyday objects as a grand piano, guitars, a coffee set, a wheelchair, and a typewriter.

He also built a series of small churches from cardboard packaging. "I needed lots of different packets," he says, "so we bought a lot of things just because of the packaging. Buying one of every item in the supermarket was fun but it did leave us with a cupboard full of food we didn't much like and couldn't tell what it was because I'd taken the wrappings off!"

Chris Gilmour's cardboard replica of a Fiat 500 car extends way beyond the simple exterior. The steering wheel, dashboard, and even the engine are modeled in precise detail.

Gilmour's cardboard typewriter is so realistic that visitors to his exhibitions are often tempted to press the keys.

It's hard to believe that these beautifully intricate 12-speed bicycles are made out of scrap cardboard packaging. Gilmour particularly enjoys creating objects that usually have moving parts—"you want to open the car door or turn the wheel on the bike, but of course you can't."

Gilmour says that he chose to re-create the famous 007 Aston Martin because "I wanted to take the idea of James Bond as this glamorous, invincible superhero and contrast it with an object made of total rubbish."

BMT 216A

Index

Page numbers in *italics* refer to illustrations

ACKNOWLEDGMENTS

COVER (l) Scott Cummins, (t/r) Althea Crome Merback; BACK COVER (l) Robert Luczun; 6–7 Tortilla Paintings © 2007 Joe Bravo; 8 AFP/
Getty Images; 9 Reuters/Amit Dave; 8–9 (t) Alex Macnaughton/Rex Features; 10 (t/l) Yara Clüver; 10–11 Althea Crome Merback; 12 www.
brickartist.com; 13 Camille Allen www.camilleallen.com; 14–15 Robert Luczun; 16 Courtesy of Pete Goldlust/Amy Mac Williamson; 17
SWNS.com; 18 (t) Gavin Bernard/Barcroft Media, (c/r, b) Mark Beekman; 19 Gavin Bernard/Barcroft Media; 20–21 Jeff Gagliardi; 24 (t)
Photocome/PA Photos; 25 (t/l, t/c) Caters News Agency Ltd/Rex Features; 24–25 (b) Hu Xuebai/ChinaFotoPress/Photocome/PA Photos; 27
(t) Reuters/Danilo Krstanovic; 26–27 (b) Wang Bin/ChinaFotoPress/Photocome/PA Photos; 28–29 Scott Cummins; 30 (t) Peter Macdiarmid/
Getty Images, (b) ChinaFotoPress/Photocome/PA Photos; 31 Chris Jackson/Getty Images; 32–33 courtesy Perugi artecontemporanea Italy

Key: t = top, b = bottom, c = center, l = left, r = right, sp = single page, dp = double page

All other photos are from Ripley Entertainment Inc.
Every attempt has been made to acknowledge correctly and contact copyright holders and we apologize in advance for any unintentional errors
or omissions, which will be corrected in future editions.